7 PRINCIPLES OF MARRIAGE: Practical Guide To Lasting Marriage.

Liam Olivia

Table of Content

Chapter 1

WHAT IS MARRIAGE

Marriage is a union of distinct individuals. It serves as a social and legal compact, also known as matrimony, that provides a partner with someone to rely on, increases closeness, and provides emotional security. Since the beginning of time, marriage has been accepted as a family and economic relationship. However, it has come a long way over the years to be acknowledged as a union of lovers who vow to remain together forever.

Marriage is a legally recognized and socially accepted relationship, typically between a man and a woman, that is governed by laws, norms, conventions, beliefs, and attitudes that outline the partners' obligations and grant status to their kids (if any). The many fundamental social and personal functions that marriage provides a structure for, including sexual gratification and regulation, the division of labor between the sexes, economic production and consumption, and the satisfaction of personal needs for affection, status, and companionship, are what is responsible for marriage's universality across different societies and cultures. Procreation, child care, education, socialization, and lineage regulation are perhaps its three most important functions. Marriage has existed in many different forms over the years.

There are many different kinds of marriages, each with a distinct function in achieving a balance between life and love. The sort of marriage, such as civil unions, interfaith unions, polygamous unions, arranged unions, marriages of convenience, and safety unions, depends on what the parties involved want from one another.

STAGES OF MARRIAGES

The Honeymoon Phase
The "honeymoon" stage of marriage begins immediately following the wedding and lasts for the next few months, perhaps extending as long as a year or two. It is universally accepted as romantic, emotional, and idealistic. The army would not enlist men during the first year of their marriage to give them time to begin establishing their marriage, a house, and a family. This stage, which is marked by passion, sexual intimacy, and infatuation, may be incredibly delicate and turbulent and fosters a sense of marital closeness.

The Phase of Adjustment
The phrase "the honeymoon's over" is not just a catchphrase! As the first stage of marriage concludes, the second one begins; it may do so gradually or abruptly, depending on the events impacting the

bride, the husband, and their future together.

In essence, the couple's obsession with one another and their brand-new, undivided love starts to fade.

This stage is enlightenment, or awakening, to the "full picture" of marriage when they are brought back into the "real world" by other responsibilities such as employment, in-laws, homemaking, child-rearing, and their growing familiarity with one another. It can cause some somber insights and "what have I gotten myself into" moments to realize that you married someone who is flawed and possibly exhibits unattractive or even dubious attributes.

The Great Escape Phase
Power battles may break out after the first three years or so when each spouse stakes out their territory and establishes their lines of defense. The spouse may only be a small

part of how each partner reinvents themselves at this point of the marriage when they start to understand they married someone with more faults than virtues. The "seven-year itch" is a part of this period and many marriage therapists now believe that some couples may experience it at a younger age, possibly at three or five years. When disappointment, arguments, and frustration take the place of the earlier passion and adaptations, the possibility of an affair is evident.

The Phase of Reevaluation
Couples often continue to adjust to their situation and one another's peculiarities well into the second decade of marriage after the first decade of marriage has ended. When there are kids around or if they have had positive role models or mentors, they start to mature. Instead of choosing to leave the marriage, they decide to recommit, assess the positives and negatives of their

union, and seek to improve family life while reestablishing their marriage.

The Phase of Growing Together
The pair may experience quiet moments throughout their second or third decade of marriage after enduring boredom, strife, and temptation thus far. Suddenly, they have another chance to rediscover one another. This is a wonderful chance for them to refocus on each other rather than juggling kids, jobs, and difficulties that come with marriage when children grow up and leave for college and one or both couples settle into fulfilling employment. As couples renew their commitment to one another, renewal ceremonies and second honeymoons are becoming increasingly popular. Keep in mind the sworn phrase, "Until death do us part."

The Midlife Conflict Stage
Women endure midlife changes through biological and emotional changes in their

40s and 50s (and occasionally in their 30s), but both sexes have the potential to go through a psychological midlife "crisis" when they reach the zenith of their careers or marriages. They suddenly notice how quickly the other half of their lives are declining. Some people become so anxious about nearing retirement and getting older that they overreact in an obsessional search for youth to prolong their "best years," at times leaving their wives in search of a younger "model."

Empty-nest syndrome can also cause problems because it causes a couple to prioritize one other over their children and comes with its own set of problems.

The Execution Phase
After a few decades, the husband and wife realize that they have successfully maintained their marriage at this point, and they are happy to continue doing so for the remainder of their lives. Some couples may

choose to do this by just reflecting on their earlier years of marriage and feeling grateful they had each other through both good and bad times. Others experience the fulfillment phase as "falling in love all over again," understanding they made the best choice in a life mate, and being thankful to have that person in their lives as they age together

. They have supported one another through good times and bad, suffered numerous setbacks, and rejoiced in life's victories. Currently, they It's possible that you won't go through each stage of marriage in the same order. Or perhaps you'll encounter stuff that aren't on this list. The essential issue is that few marriages function continuously on one level for the length of two people's whole lives after deciding to get married.

Things shift. Life takes place. There are many different situations that people go through that might affect how they feel about their partner. Even while the divorce rate today is slightly lower than it was a few years ago—around 50%—it is still too high. Couples have a higher chance of sticking together and conquering challenges in their path if they have a better awareness of what to expect and how to react in a marriage that lasts for many years.

Married people may wish to take some time to reflect on the stage of their marriage they are in and make plans on how to move forward. You will hopefully learn more about and love your partner in each stage of marriage as you go through them.

Chapter 2.

UNDERSTANDING THE DIFFERENCE BETWEEN SEX AND SEXUALITY

SEX: Sex describes a person's gender, including whether or not they have a penis or vagina.

Many of you may have observed that there is frequently a question on the form titled "Sex" when filling out various forms for school or at the doctor's office. You must select either a guy or a female. The term "sex" is frequently used to refer to sexual activity.

SEXUALITY: term "sexuality" refers to the full expression of your gender or your sexual orientation as a human. Our sexuality starts when we are born and ends when we die. Every human creature is sexual. Body image, gender identity, gender role, sexual orientation, and eroticism all have a role in how you experience sexuality .Connections, love and tenderness, and genitalia. One's sexual orientation encompasses both his or her attitudes, values, information, and actions. Sexual identity and expression are influenced by a person's families, society, culture, and religious views.

You should teach your child about sexual health as a parent, not simply sex. Personal cleanliness, good relationships, sexuality, and consent are all aspects of sexual health.The physical, mental, emotional, and social well-being of an individual all affect their sexual health. Your whole health and well-being depend on you taking care of your sexual health. Making ensuring your child has the knowledge, skills, and capacity to safeguard their health and the health of others now and in the future is part of teaching sexual health.

6 Benefit of Sex In Marriage

1.Enhances the intimacy between partners

One of the most important aspects of every relationship is intimacy. Relationships that lack intimacy frequently become unstable and fall apart, making them either impossible to heal or difficult to bring back to life. Having said that, sex is the only thing that can restore the passion and vigor in a relationship. It helps you forget the things that turn you off and it makes the couple more intimate.

2. Assures a lasting relationship

In a marriage, sexual intimacy is paramount. Initially, the relationship is held together by love and attraction, but as time passes, sex becomes more important in preserving the partnership's durability. Intimacy will be absent if there is no sexual activity.

3.Is a fantastic way to unwind

It is only normal to feel worn out and tense after a hard day at the office. One needs to know how to decompress and unwind, especially in married couples when work-life balance is so crucial. One approach is via sexual activity. It not only makes it easier for you to appreciate your partner's company, but it also calms your nerves and relieves stress.

4. It fosters an emotional link in addition to the physical one.

Hot, passionate sex can frequently result in both physical pleasure and a stronger emotional connection with your spouse. Even if your marriage may not always be going your way, you may learn a lot about what your partner is trying to tell you simply by having sex with them.

5. Maintains your attention on your relationship

Marriages frequently grow boring, and people begin exploring for other romantic partners outside of their marriages. An unhealthy sexual life may be the cause of this. Distractions are unnecessary if your partner and you have a strong physical connection. Having said that, having sex aids in maintaining attention in a relationship.

Chapter 3

Principle 1 : Love/Commitment.

At first, when all we have is each other, we pay close attention to the fundamental components of a strong and happy marriage. But as our partnership develops, "stuff" starts to assemble and takes our attention away from the fundamentals of what makes a happy marriage.

Suddenly, the assessment value of our house causes us more concern than the worth of our marriage. We frequently examine the status of our retirement account before our marriage. Or we neglect the person in our bed in favor of caring for the automobile in the garage.

Our houses and lives start to fill up with things, and soon they start to demand our money, time, and valuable energy. As a result, we don't have much left over to take care of the essentials of a happy marriage.

Wise couples understand that while having a good home, car, or retirement account may seem lovely to have, these things alone may not guarantee a happy marriage. They are aware that there are much more crucial values at stake.

They have discovered the importance of spending money, time, and effort on the following eight factors for a happy marriage:

Being committed to another person is the essence of love. In contrast to what is depicted on television, the big screen, and in romance novels, it is much more than a transitory emotion. Feelings come and go, but a sincere commitment to one person lasts a lifetime, and that is what makes a marriage healthy.

Through the good and the bad, the ups and the downs, marriage is a commitment. Commitment comes naturally when things are going well. But true love shows itself by sticking together despite difficulties. Love that is committed to a long-term relationship is known as committed love or commitment.

Is There Love Without Commitment?

Currently, commitment is out of style. Relationships without commitment, however, seem to be becoming more common. People who haven't committed exchange phrases like, "I love you, but what I mean is I want to spend the day with you. Tomorrow might bring a greater chance, and if it does, I'll seize it." This may not come as a surprise. Why not benefit from the fact that, depending on one's region, dating apps have made it quite simple to meet new people? Why pass up the opportunity to meet someone fresh who might be more interesting? Not less importantly, by simply never promising anything, one might escape responsibility for having numerous affairs at once. While there is merit in being ambivalent and keeping one's options open—I'll come back to this point at the end—I want to make the case that doing neither puts us on the road to loneliness. I want to start by defining the distinction between young love and adult love to make my case.

When we first fall in love with someone, we are largely unaware of what is going on in their head. Was she sincere when she stated she liked us too? Has she had a change of heart since Friday? He says he had fun, but is he just being polite by stating that? At this point, we frequently try to infer the other's thoughts, feelings, and interests by chatting to other individuals who are acquainted with the subject of our passion or spying on them online.

At the beginning of a relationship, nothing the other says can provide us with the confidence we need because we view the other's mind to be initially impenetrable. Everything and anything can cause us to feel insecure and jealous. We don't know each other well enough to be able to anticipate potential threats.

I'd like to leave you with some advice from a knowledgeable and senior philosopher who used to be my professor. He has a long history of contented marriage. I questioned him about marriage because I was young and had no idea what I thought about it. According to him, being married is similar to telling someone, "In this unstable world, there isn't much you can trust, but you can count on me,"

Chapter 4

Principle 2 : Sexual Fidelity.

Marriage sexual faithfulness encompasses more than just our physical selves. Our eyes, minds, hearts, and soul are also a part of it. Sexual faithfulness to our spouse is sacrificed when we focus our thoughts on dreams of a sexual nature with someone else. We give up being sexually faithful to our marriage when we share intimate emotional encounters with someone else.

Protect your sexuality every day and give it to your partner fully. Self-control and understanding of the implications are necessary for sexual faithfulness. Refuse to let anything that might jeopardize your loyalty to come in contact with your eyes, body, or heart.

10 Reason To Be Faithful To Your Partner

1.Being loyal to your partner makes them more likely to reciprocate.

2. Maintaining faithfulness helps a relationship or marriage endure. Cheating is the quickest and simplest way to end a relationship or marriage.

3. Being faithful gives you peace of mind since you don't have to watch your back or live in constant fear of saying something untrue.

4. Your sex life will be better if you are faithful. Being faithful is hot. No one feels comfortable having sex with a spouse who has been with someone else, but when your spouse knows you are faithful, they will give you amazing sex.

5. Being devoted forces you to concentrate on your marriage or relationship. You are not sidetracked, making sexual advances toward or flirting with someone else. Your love life is made healthy by your focus.

6. Why are you in that relationship or marriage if you don't want to be devoted? If you're not going to be exclusive, what's the point of committing? If you are sick of the commitment, break it off; don't keep it going while you cheat since that demonstrates how low you have descended and makes a joke of your devotion.

7. God is trustworthy; seek to imitate God.

8. People appreciate you more when you are faithful. People will respect and admire you if you maintain your integrity, rebuke anyone attempting to seduce you away from your partner, and openly demonstrate your dedication to them.

9. Being unfaithful makes you sick, not just from sexual illnesses but also from the rotting of your heart, which makes you less of the wonderful person you are in reality. Condoms cannot shield you from the deterioration of your soul.

1 There is just grief, regret, and devastation when someone is disloyal; there is no fruit, reward, or advantage. Being unfaithful feeds your ego and makes you blind.

Chapter 5

Principle 3 : Humility.

Relationships always make our flaws more obvious than anything else on earth since we all have them. The capacity to accept that you are not perfect, that you will make mistakes, and that you will want forgiveness, is a crucial component of a successful marriage. Having a superior attitude toward your partner will cause resentment and impede the development of your relationship.

Accepting the fact that you are not always correct and that others have something to contribute requires humility. Applying this idea in courtship, marriage, and the majority of other relationships is crucial.

You demonstrate humility by:

- letting go of the idea that you must impress him (or her) by being flawless.
- Admitting, at least to yourself, both your weaknesses and your talents
- creating space for the other person to express himself by attentively listening.
- putting your judge aside—at least temporarily. If his views or politics are different from yours, be curious rather than dismissive.

Humility Means Accepting Differences

When we can accept diversity, relationships flourish. Therefore, it's crucial to let go of the idea that our approach is better than the other person's and to accept the fact that, most of the time, neither of us is right or wrong when competing opinions are expressed. Simply said, we are different.

Being Humble Is a Virtue

Some individuals equate humility with frailty. However, the reverse is true. Recognizing that we don't have all the answers and resisting the want to jump in with our opinion before fully hearing what the other person has to say requires inner strength.

Learning from Others

It takes courage to be open to learning from others, particularly in our independent-minded American culture. It implies that you can resist the urge to behave rigidly and instead choose to behave more like a willow that bends with the breeze. Naturally, this does not imply that you should disregard the knowledge you already possess. It entails having the capacity to put oneself aside to make space to get to know someone by listening to him share his thoughts, feelings, hopes, and dreams while demonstrating an interest in what he has to say.

Chapter 6

Principle 4 : Patience/Forgiveness.

To forgive, one must be willing to admit that they are fallible human beings who may suffer from hurt and be injured. Additionally, it implies that you want to take control of your life and stop acting or feeling like a victim.

Because no one is perfect, a married partnership will always require patience and forgiveness. Successful couples discover how to forgive and have endless patience with one another. They do not demand perfection from their relationship and freely recognize their shortcomings. They don't bring up previous mistakes to control their partner.

And when mistakes are made, they don't try to get even or seek retribution. Forgive your partner if you're hanging onto a grudge from a previous argument. Your heart and connection will be freed by it.

five things you need to know about forgiveness in marriage.

1.Pardoning what happened is what forgiveness is.
Giving someone the benefit of the doubt does not imply that you ignore what they did or downplay the repercussions. Only until we admit our damaged sentiments can we ask for forgiveness.

You might not feel like forgiving your spouse, and when you are unable to do so, your hurt and anger fester inside of you. One of the first steps to forgiving in a marriage is having the will to do so and changing your perspective on the past to one that is more accurate.

You eventually come to understand that individuals behave in some ways that serve their interests, which aids in the processing of your own emotions.

2. **Losing oneself in forgiveness**

We should never demand an apology even though we deserve one. Giving up the urge for vengeance, blame, and anger is what forgiveness is all about. To let go of it, we must choose not to become defensive.

No matter how difficult it may seem, letting go is essential if we want to move forward with a healthy relationship. Never letting go simply makes our marriage worse.

Once your husband has apologized and begged for forgiveness, you must realize that you must forgive him. Even though it could be uncomfortable, you must express your feelings before moving forward.

Most importantly, keep in mind that forgiveness is a process that requires its own time, which you cannot always control. Take your time.

3. **Moving ahead requires forgiveness**. Numerous studies demonstrate the advantages of forgiving for our own mental and emotional well-being. It's likened to driving a car and only paying attention in the rearview mirror.

If we continue to dwell on the past, it is very difficult to move on. To move on, forgiveness entails letting go of the unpleasant moments.

4. **Trust and forgiveness are two different things**. Although it can be simple to conflate forgiveness with trust, the two things are never the same. Regaining trust may take time, and the timing may depend on how serious the offense was.

Although trust may take a while to develop, it may be destroyed in a matter of seconds.

It is possible to freely provide forgiveness while gradually restoring trust.

Women have a harder time forgetting their transgressions because they remember details better than men do. The adage "forgive and forget" is commonly known, yet it doesn't always apply to us.

Chapter 7

Principle 5 : Time.

Relationships require a time investment to be successful. not now and never will. Intentional, quality time spent together is essential for any relationship to succeed. And when quantity time is lacking, quality time rarely occurs.

The closest and most profound relationship you have should be with your spouse. As a result, it will take longer than any other relationship. Set aside sometime each day, if you can, for your spouse. Additionally, going on a date once in a while wouldn't hurt.

Being proactive in controlling the time you spend on yourself, being a couple, and being a family is one of the easiest things you can do for your relationship. A loyal spouse frequently ends up as a weary roommate when life becomes crazy. If you can't manage them, work, kids, and social commitments will take up all of your free time and more. People who put their relationships last learn how to set boundaries in their various roles and prioritize their priorities.

Couple

Many people have great memories of the start of their relationships. They recall all the encounters, excursions, and joyous times they had meeting each other. Then your life seems to be taken over by work, PTA meetings, and maintaining the lawn. Your partnership leaves you yearning. There are primarily three strategies to carve out time for your relationship. You must schedule conversations, dates, and physical connections.

Making the time to talk to your partner about your relationship can help you both feel like teammates and help you avoid future disputes. collaborating to combat the chaos of the planet. It's also crucial to schedule a dating night. Life can't be all work, so taking a night to connect and have fun makes relationships stronger. This could be anything from a walk around the local lake to a gourmet supper at a restaurant. Your relationship will get stronger if you just take a little time to rekindle your passion. It adds money to your relationship's emotional bank account so that it can survive any withdrawals you might need to make in the future.

7. Reasons Why Quality Time Masters
We have outlined fifteen factors that highlight the value of quality time spent with your partner in a relationship below. After reading this, maybe you'll be motivated to make an effort to spend more time with your partner.

1. maintains passion

You can connect with your lover on a level other than emotional and spiritual when you're together. You may feel closer to one another and maintain the fire in your relationship by making the extra effort to spend time together and improve for one another. Spending time together might help you reconnect with your mate and rekindle that passion in relationships that have lost their flame. Additionally, you'll have the chance to talk about how to handle and enhance your sexual relationship.

2. alleviates stress

There is no denying the burden of life. Juggling obligations and problems from several facets of your life are challenging. Even being in a relationship can occasionally be difficult.

But taking time out of your days to spend time with each other might be a terrific way to forget about problems and unwind. Spending time together gives couples a better opportunity of overcoming obstacles and issues that may arise.

3 makes communication better.
Spending time with your spouse or partner provides an opportunity to talk, which is a positive. The most important thing is that you can communicate with each other, even if you're just taking a walk together.

Asking your partner about their day or getting their viewpoint on a topic might help you communicate better. You don't always have to have "depth" conversations with them. These seemingly insignificant details can have a significant impact on the quality of your connection.

Making the time to talk to your partner will help you feel more like a team and prevent any future arguments that might occur.

4. Builds memories.

Taking the time out of your schedule to spend some quality time together contributes to more meaningful experiences. Going on picnics, taking a holiday trip together, or watching movies at the cinema together are moments you can look back on fondly.

Sometimes, meaningful experiences can be found in small increments of time. Stopping to watch the sunset or cracking silly jokes while cooking breakfast are little moments that pass quickly but are essential to reminding couples of the love they share for each other.

5. combats depression

Even those in committed relationships are not exempt from the effects of depression, which is a widespread mental health problem that affects many people. It's possible to have both good and bad experiences while dating, but it's never too late to talk about them and move on.

Spending time with your spouse who you suspect may be experiencing these emotions can assist ease their load and serve as a constant reminder of your love for them. Of course, it's crucial to keep in mind that if the issue persists or gets worse, a professional has to be contacted.

6. Enhances balance

Relationships do not need you to sacrifice your identity. Maintaining requires juggling your requirements and wants. Spending more time together helps you get to know each other's personalities better. By doing this, you may support one another in finding the right balance in your union.

7. Enhances intimacy

You can learn more about someone's character when you spend a lot of time with them. A person is easier to relate to and establish a connection with on a level that goes beyond just the physical the more information you have about them.

Chapter 8

Principle 6 : Integrity and faith.

Everything in a happy marriage is built on trust and honesty. However, trust takes time, unlike the majority of the other factors on this list. Selflessness, commitment, and patience can be attained in a split second, but trust always takes time. Only after several weeks, months, and years of living up to your word and carrying it through will trust be established. Start now because it will take time, and work harder if you need to rebuild trust in your relationship.

Being completely open and truthful with your spouse about both important and minor issues is what it means to be honest in a relationship. You aren't being honest if you avoid discussing issues with your partner, such as those that are bothering you in the union, actions you took that you know would make them angry, or your true feelings regarding topics you discuss. Being sincere means never disguising who you are, what you think, or how you feel from your spouse.

10 Reasons Why Honesty In Marriage Is So Important

1. Enhances trust

Why is being honest crucial? You naturally seek out the positive aspects of your relationship when you trust them.

According to a study by Redeemer University College and Northwestern University, trusting partners perceive one another as being more caring than they are.

As with love and honesty, trust and honesty complement one another. A spouse is less likely to remember unpleasant situations with their partner the more trusting they feel toward them.

Is this advantageous? We say yes as long as your spouse is kind to you and is always truthful with you.

You'll feel more secure, accepted, and loved in your relationship if you can trust your partner. Additionally, it lays a strong foundation for a bright future together.

2 Lessens anxiety among partners
Why is trust so crucial in a relationship?

Simply said, there is no worse feeling than suspecting your partner of being untruthful. You start to doubt everything when you sense that your relationship isn't being honest with you.

Do they intend to go where they say they do?
Do they cherish me?
Am I sufficient for them?
When I'm not around, what are they on their phone doing?

Many of these concerns are the result of personal fears, sometimes brought on by broken relationships in the past. Honesty between couples lowers relationship anxiety and fosters the development of trust.

3. Promotes Healthy Communication

Why is being truthful beneficial? You establish a flow of communication when nothing is stopping you from being completely honest with your spouse.

Not only will love and honesty help couples become closer and learn more about each other, but they will also make it simpler to handle disputes and prevent minor issues from becoming out of hand.

4. Builds respect

Why is being honest crucial? Sincerity with your partner is a sign of regard for them.

Because you don't want them to worry, you owe them the courtesy of informing them of your plans and expected return time. Love is not withheld in favor of frivolous games. Instead, you opened your heart to your spouse.

An honest and loving relationship depends on both of these.

Your partner is more likely to exhibit their very best traits and treat you with the same respect as they would if they felt safe and loved.

5.Creates a solid basis for love
The significance of honesty in a relationship is supported by research. According to a study that was published in the Medical Care Journal, trust is a readiness to be vulnerable that fosters another person's sense of dependability and strength.

6. It stops pointless guessing games.
Have you ever had to admit to your lover that you can't read their minds?

Or perhaps you constantly dropping critical hints in your partner's direction, but they don't seem to be picking them up?

You can avoid the frequently irritating guessing games in relationships by learning to be honest, for example, by being open and honest about your feelings, desires, and requirements.

You're open, honest, and vulnerable rather than making your spouse go through hoops or navigate a complicated relationship maze to understand where you're coming from.

Chapter 9

Principle 7 : Communication.

Healthy marriages prioritize communication between the parties. Of course, they talk about the kids' schedules, food lists, and utility costs. However, they don't end there. They also convey aspirations, worries, and concerns. Not only do they talk about the changes in the child's life, but they also talk about the changes in their hearts and souls.

Honest, open communication serves as the cornerstone for so many other items on this list, including commitment, patience, and trust, to mention a few, thus it is crucial that it not be missed.

IMPORTANCE OF COMMUNICATION IN MARRIAGE.

1. Lack of Communication Suggests Interest

You might not be able to comprehend or empathize with your spouse if you are unaware of what is going on in their life or of any potential problems they may be facing. Therefore, it is crucial to have excellent communication. Otherwise, this could gradually result in a lack of interest in one another's lives and strained relationships.

2. Greater comprehension

In addition to having a greater understanding of one another, couples who regularly converse, share their lives or communicate with one another also develop stronger bonds. There is less chance for misunderstanding or ambiguity when you comprehend your partner and the circumstances they may be facing.

3. Improved Martial Contentment

A happy and tranquil relationship is more likely to develop if you and your spouse have established good lines of communication.

Better communication leads to more pleasure in a relationship where you talk about everything and consequently fewer arguments or disagreements.

4. Greater Honesty, Integrity, and Respect
You cannot just keep expecting everything from a marriage without ever providing anything in return. Therefore, it helps to develop stronger trust in a relationship if you are honest with your spouse and provide and receive positive feedback or disclose other difficulties with complete honesty.

5. Improved Connection
Your spouse can understand your feelings and emotions when you communicate with them. We comprehend that it is not crucial to put the love and affection you have for your spouse into words. However, one of the finest methods to convey your emotions to your partner and foster a closer bond is by being vocal and expressive.

The Most Common Mistakes Married Couples Make and How to Fix Them

1.Marriage with more "me"

You and your spouse enter into a relationship when you get married. But sometimes we forget that, and your marriage starts to revolve more around you than it does around your partner. For instance, you would only arrange a vacation when you can take leave, you would only travel to places you prefer, and every year on your anniversary, you want your husband to treat you special by taking you out to dinner. All of this demonstrates that you should put your happiness or consent before that of your companion.

How to Fix

You must consider your partner's interests too. This would be possible when you communicate better with each other. Talk to your partner and know what they like or dislike, or what their idea of celebration or other such things is.

2. **Shouting At Your Spouse**

Every partnership will inevitably experience ups and downs. However, it is not acceptable to yell at or say hurtful things to your spouse if they make a mistake, regardless of how minor or serious it is. It is crucial to realize that everyone errs, and that when you yell at or reprimand your partner, you say harsh things. When there is little to no communication in a marriage, words spoken in anger might more easily hurt the other person's sentiments or emotions.

How to fix

Even if you have a good reason to be furious, resist the urge. Make cautious to convey your message subtly and without inciting hostility or hatred. The best course of action is to wait until your anger has subsided before bringing it up with your partner. The goal is to avoid making the same mistake again, not to express disapproval or sadness.

3. **Avoid competing or comparing**

Couples who are married often compare or compete with one another, which is one of the stupidest mistakes they can do. Those with comparable professional backgrounds or jobs might exhibit this error more overtly or obviously. With your partner, you could boast about your accomplishments or professional successes or disparage them for their failings or losses. It is acceptable to have healthy competition or a competitive spirit with your spouse, but you should never insult them. Additionally, poor communication in a marriage might make things worse.

How to fix.

The most important thing to realize is that, despite having different occupations, you are still one person or are bound together by love, which makes your relationship more important than anything else. Encourage your spouse when they struggle, and celebrate when they succeed. There is no room for comparison or rivalry between two people who genuinely care for one another.

Various Effective Communication Techniques to Strengthen Your Marriage

1 .Informal Communication

You talk about important subjects as well as other absurd events that occurred during the day. You enjoy chatting about some amusing things of life while laughing together. Given that you share amusing and joyful experiences with your partner, this type of communication aids in strengthening your relationship.

2. Talk About Obstacles

Every marriage experiences lows and highs, so it's critical to talk and jointly assess the positives and negative aspects of your union. Such discussions foster relationship development and support individuals in making crucial life decisions and adjustments.

3. **Life-giving Communication**
Instead of being prompted by a need or demand like the interactions stated above, this discourse is proactive. These conversations place a strong emphasis on having thoughtful discussions that cover topics like talking about your worries, desires, dreams, and hopes, among others. Included in this are meaningful discussions that can result in meaningful relationships. These are incredibly private talks that reveal details about your spouse's private life.

4. **Life-giving Communication**
Instead of being prompted by a need or demand like the interactions stated above, this discourse is proactive. These conversations place a strong emphasis on

having thoughtful discussions that cover topics like talking about your worries, desires, dreams, and hopes, among others. Included in this are meaningful discussions that can result in meaningful relationships. These are incredibly private talks that reveal details about your spouse's private life.

Guidelines for Better Communication in Your Marriage

1.Try to be more precise.

Any time you want to make a point, be sure to be explicit. Avoid waffling on the subject or bringing up irrelevant side issues. Don't generalize by using phrases like "You always say this" or "You always do this." You can end up hurting your partner rather than accomplishing your goal with this.

2. Show respect

It's crucial to treat your partner with respect no matter what kind of talk you two are having. Being a good listener demonstrates your respect for your relationship. Your lover will listen to you if you do when you have something to say.

3. **Avoid drawing hasty conclusions**

Without speaking with your partner first, avoid making assumptions or making up your narrative. Without even knowing or giving your spouse the chance to explain why they did not answer the phone, you can become upset that they did not do so. Discuss your concerns with your spouse so that you can learn the truth about their side of the tale.

4. **Talk to One Another Frequently**

No matter how busy you are or how much work needs to be done, make sure you set aside some time each day to have a meaningful chat with your spouse. Get crazy or goofy and laugh heartily with each other if you can't think of anything to say. To keep the love in the relationship flowing, it is crucial to interact with your partner frequently.

5. Avoid Being Defensive

It's crucial to listen carefully and without getting defensive if your partner has to air grievances or difficulties against you. It can be challenging for your partner to expose their faults in front of you. Instead of being overly defensive about the whole thing, make sure you pay attention and take appropriate action to resolve the problem.

www.ingramcontent.com/pod-product-compliance
Lightning Source LLC
Chambersburg PA
CBHW070605160726
48003CB00005B/2123